RAPHAEL

RAFFAELE MONTI

GROSSET & DUNLAP
Publishers - New York

First American edition published 1967 by Grosset & Dunlap, Inc.
All rights reserved
Translated from the Italian by Caroline Beamish
Translation copyright © 1967 by Thames and Hudson, London
Copyright © 1966 by Sadea Editore, Firenze
Library of Congress Catalog Card Number: 67-24228

Printed and bound in Italy

Life

Raphael was born in Urbino on 6 April 1483, the son of Giovanni Santi, one of the most esteemed painters and thinkers at the court of Urbino. Although Santi was already dead by 1494 it seems likely that his influence on his son's education had already made itself felt: it was reflected particularly in his predilection for the highly analytical modes of thought which, since Piero della Francesca and Laurana, were current in literary and artistic circles at the court of Urbino. After the death of his father, Raphael left the city of his birth, possibly under the tutelage of Evangelista da Piandimeleto, a pupil and trusted friend of his father. Piandimeleto probably collaborated with Raphael in the execution of his first commissioned work, the *Altarpiece of St Nicholas of Tolentino.*

By this time (about 1500) it is almost certain that he was a pupil of Pietro Perugino, who was his tutor and guide in both artistic and intellectual matters; numerous commissions followed the completion of the San Nicola altarpiece, and the young Raphael achieved immediate fame. He soon recognized the need of escaping from the limitations of Umbrian painting towards Florentine ideas and techniques, already partly known to him through the teaching of Perugino.

In October 1504, when he had finished the *Marriage of the Virgin* for the church of San Francesco, in Città di Castello, he arrived in Florence with a letter of introduction from Giovanni Feltria. This move did not sever his relations with Umbria completely, as he had left certain commissions there unfinished (*Altarpiece of the Sisters of San Antonio, Ansidei Madonna*). In Florence he was accepted at once into the neo-Platonic circle, now reestablished after the Savonarola crisis. He became intimate with painters such as Fra' Bartolomeo (also a pupil of Perugino), and before long, with the completion of the series of *Madonnas* and *Holy Families,* culminating in the magnificent *Madonna of the Baldachin,* he became the leading figure in Florentine painting during those early years of the fifteenth century. Leonardo da Vinci and Michelangelo being almost perpetually absent from the city, very young painters such as Andrea del Sarto, Franciabigio, and even Pontormo modelled themselves on Raphael's example. During this period, in short visits to Umbria, he completed the *Deposition* for Atalanta Baglioni (now in the Galleria Borghese) and the frescoes in San Severo, Perugia, of *Christ in majesty with Saints.*

Between 1507 and 1509 he reached a turning-point in his career which has never been satisfactorily explained: it may possibly have been due to the fact that the work of completing the frescoes in the Salone of the Palazzo Vecchio (left unfinished by Michelangelo and Leonardo) was not assigned to him; or, more likely, to his awareness of the crisis, now becoming acute, in the cultural and political life of Florence. In any case, Raphael moved to Rome. In 1509 he received a salary as a court painter. Under the protection of Pope Julius II he began the decoration of the Stanze in the Vatican in 1511: his frescoes in the Stanza della Segnatura established him as a direct rival to Michelangelo (who was then painting the ceiling in the Sistine Chapel), and as a key figure in neo-Platonic circles in Rome; literary members of the neo-Platonic circles included Cardinal Bembo, Cardinal Bibbiena, Castiglione, Aretino and Cardinal Inghirami. In the same year he painted the fresco of *Galatea* for Agostino Chigi on the wall of his villa, now known as the Farnesina, and *The Prophet Isaiah* in Sant'Agostino; probably at the same time, also for Chigi, he was drawing plans for the chapel of Santa Maria del Popolo.

Between 1511 and 1514 he painted the frescoes in the Stanza di Eliodoro in the Vatican. When Julius II died, Raphael remained in favour with his successor, the Medici Pope Leo X, who gave a new importance to the study of ancient Rome which was to make a strong impression on Raphael.

Having become a kind of cultural dictator at the Papal Court (which was why Michelangelo chose to return to Florence), at the death of Bramante in 1514, Raphael was given the position of architect in the rebuilding of Saint Peter's. During these years his activity as ar architect in-

4

tensified; besides the Chigi chapel, he built the Palazzo Caffarelli Vidoni, and rebuilt the Palazzo Branconio dell'Aquila, which had been destroyed. In 1515 he was commissioned to make cartoons for the tapestries in the Sistine Chapel; in 1516 he was appointed Curator of Roman Antiquities. In 1517 the Stanza dell'Incendio was completed; Raphael's part in this was to provide drawings, as he had for the Logge in the Vatican and the Loggia di Psiche in the Farnesina during the same year. On 6 April 1520, his birthday, he died after a violent fever which lasted seven days. Princely homage was paid to him: his body lay in state in the Vatican beneath the unfinished *Transfiguration* which he had started in 1519, and was buried in the Pantheon.

Works

Besides the various paintings that are attributed to Raphael but are not definitely by him, such as the small fresco showing the *Madonna in the House of her Birth*, in Urbino, or the exquisite *Madonna della Misericordia* in Città di Castello, which bears a strong resemblance to works by Piero della Francesca, Raphael's first recorded commission was the *Altarpiece of St Nicholas of Tolentino*, painted for the Church of Sant'Agostino in Città di Castello, and ordered on 10 December 1500. Three fragments of this painting survive, and also a series of beautiful drawings, now in the Musée Vicar, Lille.

Research into the early years of Raphael's working life must be based on the examination of a group of paintings which, although they cannot be given an exact date, were certainly painted during the formative years, before Raphael's visit to Florence in 1504. This group includes the *Resurrection,* in São Paolo, Brazil (*pl. 1*), the altarpiece of the *Coronation of the Virgin* (*pl. 2*), in the Vatican Gallery, the *Trinity* in the Pinacoteca in Città di Castello, the *Solly Madonna* in the Staatliche Museen, Berlin, *St Sebastian* in the Accademia Carrara, Bergamo (*pl. 3*), the *Mond Crucifixion* in the National Gallery, London, and finally the *Marriage of the Virgin* now in the Brera, Milan, signed and dated 1504 (*pls 4-5*).

The attribution of this series of paintings to Raphael is beyond reasonable doubt; his vocabulary and his mind are revealed in them with great clarity. Already by this time his mind seems to have been exceptionally mature; a proposition was stated at the very outset which, notwithstanding later digressions, was never to be gainsaid in all his brief, meteoric career. His appropriation of the characteristics of the artistic milieu in which he was brought up stands out clearly; even if there were no record of it elsewhere, these paintings would establish the relationship between the young Raphael and Perugino beyond reasonable doubt. This relationship was to remain a feature of Raphael's paintings until the so-called Florentine period. It is often regarded by critics as nothing more than the necessary iconographic borrowings of a very young pupil. To my mind it is more illuminating to examine the relationship without regard to the limits that were imposed on Perugino's style by, in the first place, his Florentine contemporaries. Whilst I recognize the obvious change in the works painted during Perugino's old age, it seems to me extremely difficult to understand Raphael's career without taking into account the fact that Perugino was his guide not only in the acquisition of an exceptional painting technique, but also in matters of thought. Raphael's cultural education included the tremendous inheritance of Piero della Francesca, whose influence remained very much alive in artistic circles in Urbino; on the other hand his teacher would have expounded to him the disquieting theories of the neo-Platonic Accademia in Florence. For Raphael the experience of Piero di Cosimo, the late Botticelli and Verrocchio made reconciliation with the rules set out by Careggi difficult; after the Savonarola upheaval these rules had been laid down again almost exactly as they were before.

If we pause for a moment to consider Perugino's Roman frescoes, and to recall the distinction in them between the figures and the scene in which they are placed, even though the proportions and perspective are not confused, in the Sala del Cambio, in Perugia, for example, finished by Perugino in 1500, we find one of the clearest statements of the relationship between the artist and neo-Platonism. He takes as subjects moral and religious allegories, giving the figures in the allegories the faces of classical heroes; religious and pagan scenes are given equal importance. Even if the participation of the young Raphael in his master's work is regarded as most improbable, it is nevertheless clear that he had first-hand knowledge of it. If we take a work by Raphael of the same date for comparison, such as the *Resurrection*, now in São Paolo, there is no denying the distinction between the figures and their surroundings, or the statuesque quality of the figures themselves, isolated in space as if in a solid element. Raphael tackles the problem of space in the same way as it was later to be tackled (with even more determination) in the paintings of the Florentine School of San Marco, and in particular by Fra' Bartolomeo and Mariotto Albertinelli, with results which were to be of great importance to Italian painting in the sixteenth century. Even as early as this Raphael allowed the important lessons learned from Perugino to pass through an extremely fine filter before making use of them himself: the son of Giovanni Santi, educated in Urbino, ' the centre of mathematics and the abstract arts during the Renaissance ' (Chastel), very soon adopted a selective approach with regard to his mentor, submitting certain of his basic tenets (without denying their validity) to a rigorous spatial re-organization in which his overriding concern is with proportion. Reared on the teachings of Piero della Francesca, Alberti and Laurana, Raphael adopted (from Bramante) the creed of symmetry, and with it Bramante's ideals of space and proportion, closely linked, in conceptual terms, with the theory of Godhead propounded by Cusano.

Although this is to a certain extent obvious in the spherical composition of the *Solly Madonna,* or in the immutable harmony of the *Christ* of Tosio Martinengo, Raphael's true voice speaks with its full linguistic and theoretical weight in the *Marriage of the Virgin*, in the Brera (*pls 4-5*). The iconographic ties between the *Marriage* and Perugino's *Giving of the Keys*, in the Sistine Chapel, are well known; they are particularly obvious in Raphael's adoption of the temple, in the style of Bramante, in the background, and in the linking of this and the group of figures in the foreground by the device of dividing up the floor into geometrical squares. But these iconographic references only serve to throw into even stronger relief Raphael's rejection of and departure from Perugino's ideas. One can see how the architectural detail plays a key role in the structure of this long painting with its arched top; the temple is at once the point at which the lines of perspective meet and the axis of a circular area of space. The geometrical division of space, Raphael's hallmark, is used to place the group of figures in the foreground. Just as the temple is placed at the centre of a series of horizontal circles which comprehends the whole canvas, so from a point immediately above the ring which Joseph is putting on to Mary's outstretched hand there springs another series of concentric circles which also comprehend the whole structure of the painting on a vertical plane. The organization of space, dictated by the central position of the temple, is unexpectedly turned upside down and a new arrangement laid down by the vision in the foreground; the two principal axes (one in the temple and the other passing through the ring) meet in the composition of the picture at a perfect right angle. The rhythmic proportions of the individual figures and the view of the background through the doorway of the temple underline a complex symmetrical arrangement of space with strong spherical suggestions. The schema could be called cosmic; through it Raphael illustrates his understanding of the language of Bramante, and at the same time reaffirms, though with less attention to metaphysics, the rules of Piero della Francesca.

In the same year in which this masterpiece was signed (1504), Raphael was in Florence. As will have been gathered from what has already been said, the arrival of the young Raphael in the Florence of the Medici took place at a time when his taste and his pictorial and cultural orientation were already firmly established. In Florence Raphael seems, perhaps because of sharing a common artistic paternity in Perugino, to have become acquainted at once with the painters of the School of San Marco, and to have shared their models. The relationship between Raphael and Fra' Bartolomeo has often been over-emphasized and distorted to the extent of suggesting that the young provincial painter depended on the friar, already by then a mature and well-known painter. Their relationship has been further falsified by the erroneous dating of two important paintings, painted during this time, the *Three Graces,* at Chantilly, and the *Vision of a Knight* in the National Gallery, London (*pl. 7*). These works, often placed at the outset of Raphael's career in Urbino, are in fact valuable documents, both historically and artistically, painted by Raphael at the start of his years in Florence. The group of the *Three Graces* is well known to have been taken' from a Roman bas-relief discovered at about the turn of the century and sent in 1502 to Cardinal Passerini. Niccolò Fiorentino cast a celebrated medallion of the same group, and the symbolism of the Three Graces was close to the heart of neo-Platonic culture, particularly in Florence where it was used over and over again. We know that the young Raphael, at the beginning of his Florentine career, became involved at once in the lively arguments of the neo-Platonic Accademia and painted (if Chastel's theory is correct, as I believe it to be) a series of mythological scenes (see the note to the *Vision of a Knight,* p. 29).

Philosophical symbolism apart, the stylistic elements which link these two small canvases directly with details already examined in the *Marriage of the Virgin* in the Brera may be listed as follows: perfect spatial relationships between structural elements, the identification of the outward surface rhythms of the picture with the inward sense of proportion and spatial organization, the integration of the figures into the organization of the whole, and the significant part played by the landscape. Raphael's rejection of Perugino's models, and his rejection of the isolated figures found in the composition of paintings by Fra' Bartolomeo (the altar-pieces recorded by Longhi included) could not be more marked. It becomes even clearer when two paintings, whose themes and composition are more closely linked to the style of Fra' Bartolomeo, are examined: the *Ansidei Madonna* and the *Madonna of St Nicholas of Tolentino,* both completed soon after Raphael's arrival in Florence, but certainly started before he set out.

Fra' Bartolomeo's floating figures, even when placed in a painting with a circular construction, are suspended in an element quite different from Raphael's carefully and immutably measured space: in Raphael's *Madonna of St Nicholas of Tolentino,* as in his *Marriage of the Virgin,* the concentric circles emanating from the right foot of the Holy Child are grafted to the centrally placed group of the throne and figures, this group being encircled by the arch of the canopy which perfects the sphere. The circles are spaced from foreground to background through the architectural details and figures. The exactness of the placing of architectural details, and the extreme clarity and brightness of the colours, make this altarpiece a perfect foil for the tender beauty of the *Ansidei Madonna.* Here we may as well abandon iconographic comparisons with Umbrian or Florentine works (from Fra' Bartolomeo to Rafaellino del Garbo); the wonderful luminosity of the painting creates its own space and measure, and situates the figures, at once isolating them and bringing them together; the light establishes time and place in a way which is supremely emotional in appeal yet which is abstract in conception, in the tradition of the greatest and most metaphysical paintings of Piero della Francesca (*pl. 6*).

It is certain that while in Florence Raphael, lively and alert as he was, must have been aware of the extraordinary influence that the style of Leonardo da Vinci was having, and not only in Florence. This is not to suggest that his awareness was an inevitable historical development (this would be absurd, and particularly in the case of someone like Raphael, whose intellectual development was so coherent and self-sufficient); it was an active recognition of a development which attacked the basic tenets to which Raphael subscribed. He could never give full acceptance to the idea of space infinitely multiplied, nor to the destruction of the traditional modular system which this idea carried with it. Even when he borrows iconographic and pictorial details from Leonardo one is conscious of his awareness of the problem, and aware that a careful selection has been made. For example in the *Terranova Madonna* (Kaiser-Friedrich-Museum, Berlin) the face and the attitude of the Madonna clearly show their derivation from the *Virgin of the Rocks;* the treatment of light also obviously stems from a study of Leonardo's work; the light fades away very gently, quivering between light and darkness. But the choice of a circular canvas, and the way it is divided up into equal parts by the balustrade; the arrangement of the component parts around the axis of the index finger on the right hand of the principal figure; the unexplained gap between the heavily draped knee in the foreground and the head of the figure of Mary (unexpectedly placed between huge expanses of carefully measured space) – all these show that Raphael basically eschewed Leonardo's ideas. The Madonna's hand, poised in the half-light, is a kind of pointer to the orderly arrangement of space.

Raphael re-states his case against Leonardo in a series of exquisitely lyrical masterpieces: the themes were ones he was to use over and over again, the Madonna and Child and the Holy Family.

The first and most famous was the painting of the Virgin and Child known as the *Madonna of the Grand Duke.* Here the echoes of Leonardo are confined to the position and carriage of the Madonna. From the point of view of composition this is one of Raphael's most complex works; the perfect symmetry of the mother and child, based on a circle, is suddenly dramatically broken by the tilting of the Virgin's head towards the left, from whence it is brightly lighted by a strong source of light (*pls 10-11*). The theme of mother and child is perfectly interpreted in the small *Cooper Madonna,* the *Tempi Madonna (pl. 13),* and the *Orleans Madonna*: in order to introduce variation Raphael re-arranges the figures and views them from different angles. Further consideration of Leonardo's style and his solution of spatial problems must surely have preceded the painting of the groups with the Madonna and Child and St John, which show full figures and are constructed on a triangular rather than a circular basis. These include the *Esterhazy Madonna* (Budapest Museum), the so-called *Belle Jardinière* in the Louvre (*pl. 14*), the *Madonna of the Goldfinch* in the Uffizi (*pl. 15*), the *Madonna and Child with St John* in the Museum in Vienna, and lastly the *Madonna and Child with*

11

St John, St Joseph and St Elizabeth (known as the *Canigiani Madonna*) now in Munich (*pls 16-17*).

The first of these groups, the *Esterhazy Madonna,* borrows its perfectly circular composition from the little *Cooper Madonna;* the way in which the figures are so firmly yet harmoniously linked to one another recalls similar usages in the work of Leonardo, from the *Benois Madonna* to the *St Anne* cartoon. Yet even though the sacred group is enclosed in a wide architectonic circle, the composition of the group is pyramidal; the different shapes are brought together by the intricately organized space which lies between them. Raphael modulates his space and, unlike Leonardo, paints figures that are in proportion to the landscape they occupy; the relationship between figures and landscape is made very clear. He re-states this relationship in the three extraordinary masterpieces which followed: the Vienna *Madonna,* the *Madonna of the Goldfinch* and *La Belle Jardinière* (*pls 14-15*). The setting of the groups in their scenery is absolutely accurate; the spectator's eye roves unchecked over the group of figures; he imagines for a moment that the story they tell is a geometrical abstraction, and that the arrangement was coincidental and just happened to be chosen at the psychological moment. The dazzling perfection of the scene lifts it above mere historical narration, and permits the expression of the deepest and most secret feelings. The sedate, triangular cluster of figures glories in its architectonic arrangement; the figures are linked by the tenderest emotional tension. The landscape backgrounds, so perfectly perspective (they are the visible portion of the sphere which encircles the group, in perfect proportion, far beyond the edges of the canvas) are paeons of praise to nature. The Elysian fields in which Raphael places his holy groups are on a human scale and seen in everyday terms; this fond vision of a familiar landscape expresses all Raphael's religious feeling without ever becoming arid and cerebral. In these paintings Raphael, with that sublime intuition which only the young Andrea del Sarto among his Florentine contemporaries was ever to understand, investigates and establishes the time of day making the movements and the expressions of the figures consistent with the early evening or the first light of dawn: the feeling of serenity and the scents and sounds are almost physically apprehensible. Having reached a state of total abstraction the poet may invent a new natural order of his own, based on his own feelings and emotions; his system goes beyond the structural schemes imposed by the neo-Platonists to become an isolated and unrepeatable moment in the history of the development of the human soul.

The culmination of Raphael's intellectual progress, the *Canigiani Madonna* (*pls 16-17*), suggests fresh and even more complicated ideas; yet its composition directly approaches the composition of the painting which I described at the beginning of this account, the *Marriage of the Virgin* in the Brera.

The halo above St Joseph's head, which is the apex of a triangle whose base is the line of buildings in the background, accentuates the perfect circle upon which the group of figures is based. The frontal view of the figures follows a circular plan as well: the line which passes through the two *putti* follows the ample curve of the body of the Madonna towards the standing figure of St Joseph. The body of the Virgin reveals Raphael's nascent interest in the work of Michelangelo, and this is confirmed in the highly organized composition of the *Baglioni Deposition*, in the Galleria Borghese (*pls 18-23*).

It was during these months that Raphael painted the marvellous pair of *Portraits of Agnolo and Maddalena Doni*, now in the Uffizi (*pls 28-29*). In one of the Florentine houses of this noble family was to be found Michelangelo's famous *Doni Tondo*, also now in the Uffizi. Raphael had been until this time familiar only with the cartoons for the *Battle of Cascina*, of Michelangelo's painted works, and probably he did not share the general admiration for their massive proportions. Now however he became deeply aware of the tautness and immutability of the circular picture, exemplified by the *Doni Tondo*; here the portico in the background is the architectural counterpart of the tightly knit group of figures in the foreground.

Raphael may have become emotionally involved with the *Doni Tondo* in the course of his work on the placing of the figures in his *Baglioni Deposition*; an early design for this turns back to Peruginesque themes, with strong reminders of Fra' Bartolomeo. The result of his pondering of the work of Michelangelo can be seen in a marvellous drawing for the complete picture (*pl. 19*); here perspective and space are measured to the last millimetre. For Raphael drawing was a way of experimenting with detail so that in the final composition everything would be exactly right. His figures were initially drawn as skeletons, placed in a position which was anatomically right; they were then clothed with flesh and with drapery strictly according to the capacity of their bone-structure (*pls 20-21*). Although these drawings were semi-scientific in intention, this does not prevent their being masterpieces in their own right; drawing was now the most direct medium for the expression of Raphael's pictorial ideas.

The final structural scheme of the *Deposition* is extremely complex; two violently contrasted groups of figures (those carrying the body of Christ and those surrounding the fainting figure of the Virgin Mary) are fused into a single entity by being encircled by an imaginary line whose axis would be the left hand of the central bearer. Around the circumference of the principal circle a series of lesser circles revolve, like small chapels round a nave; the two most clearly defined are on either side, one on the left made by the heads of the bearers, one on the right by the heads of the group around the Virgin. The landscape between the two circles seems to depend from them (*pls 18, 22-3*).

Inside the broad, dramatic structure of the painting little references and correspondences catch the eye. Viewpoints shift restlessly. The confrontation between the wide open group of bearers and the tightly closed little group around the Virgin is tragic, and in particular the pious lady kneeling down who is twisting right round to support the collapsed Madonna, a clear testimony to Raphael's familiarity with the *Doni Tondo,* from which it is a bold (and most original) plagiarism. Raphael used Michelangelo's dynamic composition to the full, discarding anything he had no use for, and fitting the figure perfectly into his intricate schema. And just as in some of his *Holy Families* the borrowed figures are given new serenity and meaning, here the dramatic impact of the Michelangelesque figure seems just as fresh.

It was during this period that Raphael moved to Rome and was commissioned by Julius II to begin the decoration of some of the rooms in the Vatican, beginning with the library, later to be called the Stanza della Segnatura. We know that these decorations had previously been entrusted to another group of artists, including Sodoma, Lorenzo Lotto and Baldassare Peruzzi. According to some art historians certain of the paintings in the vaulted ceiling owe their conception and execution to Sodoma. It is positively known, however, that when the Pope saw the extraordinary skill of the young painter from Urbino he discharged all the other artists and put the entire work into Raphael's hands. It was an extraordinary flash of intuition by someone who at the same time was pressing Michelangelo to undertake the decoration of the roof of the Sistine Chapel.

In the Stanza della Segnatura Raphael gave full reign to his imagination and brought all his earlier experience into play, transforming the chamber beyond recognition. It was the first time that he had had to paint a room of any size, and he tackled it by using the shape of the room and the divisions of the ceiling as a basis for the layout of his paintings, accepting them as limitations rather than trying to disguise them. The two openings, the window and the door, are used as part of the overall design. The window is used as a reference for the perspective schema, the door as a support for a heavy archway which in its turn supports the steep hillside where the Virtues are portrayed. Underneath the frescoes there was an inlaid wooden dado by Fra' Giovanni da Verona – this was traditionally part of the decorations of a small study during the renaissance. It was however removed in about 1540, which was a pity because its pattern of geometrical symbols must have accentuated the cosmic symmetry of the whole. Once the eye had appreciated the intricate inlay it would move upwards to the two grandiose visions, the *Dispute over the Holy Sacrament* and the *School of Athens.*

The depth of expression which Raphael gives in these frescoes to the humanist state of mind has been definitively

15

The Stanza della Segnatura. Above: Dispute over the Holy Sacrament.
Below: Parnassus (see p. 33)

shown by Chastel; although the painter had been advised by Giovio, and no doubt by the Pope himself, he plainly exposes himself here as privy to the tenets of neo-Platonism. The relationship between myth and religion is demonstrated to perfection, through symbols and confrontations between participant figures. The *speculum doctrinale* is presented to the spectator with faultless logic.

All the pomps of neo-Platonism would not be enough however to lift these paintings above a clear exegesis of contemporary cultural divisions, were they not the work of a great genius, one of the greatest narrative painters of all time. What is so overwhelming about them is Raphael's complete control both of ideas and of their lyrical expression in painting, and indeed his fusion of the two. His genius lies, here as in the works of his youth, in his bringing to life symbols and abstractions with the utmost lyricism. The *Dispute* (*pls 30-3*) is possibly Raphael's greatest achievement: the painting is fitted into its allotted space in the room, as part of the whole, yet it is a living single organism. Like a huge side chapel adjoining a centrally-planned church, it belongs, and yet is autonomous. And like a satellite, launched by the movement of its parent system, it generates its own movement and becomes independent. In this painting, as in all the youthful works, there is a symbolic and structural centre: the Host is the point at which the perpendicular lines of perspective converge and it is the centre of a series of concentric circles which cover the whole fresco. Through the Host and the stem of the chalice lies the central axis around which rotate the three symbols of the Trinity, each enclosed in its own smaller circle, united in their movement round the axis, yet divided from one another. Around this axis the huge structure, of which the nave with figures that we can see is only a section, also gravitates. The axis lies in the middle of the chamber and it is identical with that of the *School of Athens*, whose structure is analogous.

This very complex spatial organization covers every detail of the painting, and perhaps unexpectedly is responsible for the overwhelming poetic effect of the work. Perhaps a useful comparison would be the analogous phenomenon to be found in certain passages of Bach's *Art of Fugue*: the subject matter which he takes to work on becomes abstracted, that is to say it becomes free from the dross left by previous experience, thus becoming a totally purified field of endeavour, in which alone the creation of perfection is possible. This does not exclude human passions, but these are overcome by a process of rationalization until a state of serenity is reached which itself responds to the motions of the human heart, and which recognizes human passion and human drama without being disrupted by them. Man and his symbols are brought face to face.

Just as a landscape may miraculously stretch beyond the horizon, the life that we see in the next painting, the *School of Athens* (*pls 34-7*), stretches beyond the huge architectural structure (this shares the central plan of the *Dispute* and is another exact section of a sphere). The presence of the influence of Bramante in this picture, the echoes of Piero della Francesca and of Michelangelo's ceiling of the Sistine Chapel, all connect in some way with the final additions to the painting: the figure of Democritus, and in the foreground a portrait of Michelangelo. The architectural setting of this picture corresponds to the great arch in the section containing the *Dispute*, but here the design of the building is shown far more clearly. Inside the building the ' heroes of reason ' are portrayed with impressive characterization. Raphael includes himself in their number, one of the figures in the right-hand foreground; Michelangelo and Leonardo can be found as well. This then is painting used as an intellectual statement.

From the moment of his arrival in Rome Raphael increasingly affirmed an attitude which was to become more and more important as the years passed, and which has been almost entirely misunderstood by students of his work: this was his rejection of the idea of autography. In Raphael's estimation a picture could be planned and have its composition carefully laid out by himself: if the actual painting were then left to pupils and assistants to execute, this would not diminish the value of the work in the least. For this reason, when he was asked by Dürer to send him a sample of his drawing, Raphael sent off to Nuremberg a drawing by Giulio Romano which was based on an idea by Raphael.

This was certainly not out of lack of consideration for his German colleague. The ethical and theoretical implications of what he had done were certainly clear to him, and were very probably fully appreciated and shared by Dürer himself. In spite of the continual cross-references in their works, it is clear, in fact, that the intellectual path that Raphael followed differs widely from the paths of Leonardo and Michelangelo, though all three shared a common heritage of Florentine neo-Platonism.

The paintings in the Stanza della Segnatura are in fact probably the last works that Raphael completed on his own (discounting the usual practice of employing apprentices to help hurry the painting along). Two masterpieces, painted at this time, the *Aldobrandini Madonna* (now in London) and the *Alba Madonna* (now in Washington) were also single-handed works. There are some splendid portraits and small paintings which date from about this time in which the work of Raphael's pupils was not very extensive, but nevertheless always to be found. One extremely important painting, the *Foligno Madonna* (*pls 54-5*), painted immediately after the frescoes in the Stanze, presents a complicated problem: certain famous artists who were not members of Raphael's close entourage have been linked with its execution (see the note to the painting, p. 35).

The decoration of the chamber known as the Stanza d'Elio-doro was probably started in 1511: in this room, possibly at the suggestion of the Pope, the direct interventions of God in the history of mankind are portrayed.

The first fresco to be painted was almost certainly the picture of *The Expulsion of Heliodorus from the Temple* (*pls 41-3*). Here the subject is highly dramatic, and Raphael's narrative ability is given ample scope. He re-uses the centralized architectural schema, but disposes the figures in the schema with great vigour, creating two circular centres of dramatic focus, on either side of the foreground. The painting was mainly carried out by pupils, Raphael reserving for himself only a small area in the left hand corner where, with a nice touch of wit, we see Julius II, carried on his throne by Giulio Romano and Marcantonio Raimondi, watching the mythical event. The tonal difference between this corner and the rest of the fresco suggests that the portrait was painted as Julius II contemplated the scene which he had suggested to Raphael (*pl. 41*).

A moment of relaxation from Raphael's usual stringent architectural standards can be found in the upper part of the *Mass of Bolsena* (*pls 45-7*). The lapse is marvellously resolved in the slightly off-centre placing of the semi-circular choir-stall and the relationship this creates between the heavy altar, the two kneeling figures and the decentralized axis of the window underneath. The spectator's eye will inevitably be drawn to the lower right-hand section and the dramatic portraits of the Swiss Guards; they seem to be the climax of the action in the picture. This group and the corresponding group of members of the Papal Court in the *Expulsion of Heliodorus* can be seen as the focal points of their respective pictures, the openings through which the spectator gains entry into the other world portrayed in these paintings. In *Leo I forcing Attila to a halt* (*pl. 44*) and the sublime *Liberation of St Peter* (*pls 48-51*), the spectator is drawn into their orbit in the same way, and led breathlessly through a series of rotations and oblique angles. The *Liberation* is one of the key paintings in the history of art; the light, beating in on the solid figures from behind, shows the careful drawing of the forms, and seems to be the source of visions rising from the darkest depths of the soul. Piero della Francesca and Masaccio may be the great painters to whom in these days we feel most drawn (and the genesis of the *Liberation* can be traced back to their works), but our feeling for them is a direct result of the cultural thesis advanced by Raphael in the Stanza della Segnatura.

At the same period as these frescoes Raphael painted a series of canvases which were still largely his own work. Included were masterpieces such as the *Portrait of Castiglione* in the Louvre, the *Portrait of Cardinal Inghirami* in the Pitti (*pl. 69*), the *Madonna of the Chair* (*pl. 57*) and its variant (or predecessor) the *Madonna of the Fish* in the Prado (*pl. 71*) and the *Sistine Madonna* (*pl. 56*).

The *Madonna of the Chair* and the *Sistine Madonna* are certainly the most interesting non-fresco works of this period of Raphael's stylistic development. The first re-states the old

The Stanza di Eliodoro. Above: Leo I forcing Attila to a halt.
Below: Liberation of St Peter (see p. 34)

Florentine puzzle, the circular painting or *tondo* (a puzzle obviously classical in origin), and solves it with impressive skill and ease; the space around the figures is almost non-existent, and the figures themselves are linked together in perfect circular motion. Like a reflection in a convex mirror the sphere seems to protrude towards the spectator. The clever solution of the puzzle is supported by marvellous painting, here and in the *Sistine Madonna*. The latter was painted on canvas for the high altar in the church of the monks of San Sisto in Piacenza, and was intended to portray the Virgin appearing as a vision. The vision was to be a focal point from all parts of the nave; the arrangement of the drapery echoed the patterns of the architecture around it so that the roof appeared to have opened to admit the divine vision. The figure is constructed according to the Golden Section, yet it has a subtle vigour and urgency, an airy majesty and the total abstraction of a vision. This is the last large painting entirely attributable to Raphael. The *Lady with a Veil* (*pl. 72*) and the *Vision of Ezekiel* (*pl. 68*) in the Pitti, and the *Portrait of Leo X between two Cardinals* in the Uffizi (*pls 52-53*), are the last great works in which Raphael's part, albeit a small one, can be identified. The large number of works painted in the few years that remained until his death were entirely, or almost entirely, executed by his pupils. Even in the Stanza dell'Incendio, painted between 1514 and 1517, apart from the plan of the component parts and certain beautiful sections in the fresco which gives its name to the room, Raphael's hand is hardly detectable. The *Fire in Borgo* (*pls 62-5*) is nevertheless a masterpiece of the School of Raphael, and a seminal work in the history of sixteenth-century painting. Raphael's usual plan of composition has been developed: the perfectly regular central plan is still there, the section we can see dependent on a perspective system centred on the rose-window of the tympanum of the church in the background. But in this rationalized space the story unfolds around architectural protrusions, some of which are in motion, like the high wall on the left (almost hidden by the splendid figure of the young man climbing down from it), some holding firm, like the colonnade on the right between whose pillars the magnificent file of women passes. The buildings play an unprecedentedly important part in the narrative action; this is a new departure and was to be a very influential one.

It was also the first instance of the use of a massive 'monumental' setting, brought in by Raphael on the strict advice of the Papal Court which, under the leadership of Leo X, was trying hard to Latinize contemporary classical learning; hitherto the neo-Platonists had relied on the Greek classical world for their inspiration. The Greek ideal proportions, which had been rediscovered and revived by the Florentines in the fifteenth century, and which Raphael had used particularly frequently in his paintings, gave way now to the proportions of ancient Rome; these introduced a more majestic and dramatic use of space, and in effect were the occasion of the collapse of the proportional schemes that had been in use until this time.

Naturally this fundamental change of composition is more noticeable in these later works by the School of Raphael because of the absence, in the execution, of the guiding hand of the master, who was capable of turning an abstract intellectual proposition into pure poetry. Very often the hasty way in which his ideas seem to have been translated into painting (the poor state of preservation is partly to blame for this) makes them difficult to identify, and this is the case in the other three frescoes in the Stanza dell'Incendio. Nevertheless his interpretation of imaginary archaeological scenes in frescoes painted immediately after these is marvellous. These include the decorations in the Farnesina and the Logge in the Vatican (1515-17). Yet here, quite apart from the sections which were certainly executed by a group of painters including Giulio Romano, Penni and Giovanni da Udine, even the composition and preliminary cartoons may not be attributable to Raphael.

Another important series, in spite of the determining presence in their composition of the work of Giulio, Penni and Giovanni da Udine, are the cartoons for the tapestries intended to hang on the wall beneath the fifteenth-century frescoes in the Sistine Chapel. Of course the whole cycle does not achieve the same high level of expression. The

Punishment of Elymas, for example, in spite of the magnificence of its plan and the rhythmic arrangement of space
around the figure of the seated emperor, is simply one of
the most typical examples of the ' monumental ' approach to
composition which is characteristic of Raphael's last works.
The *Healing of the Cripple,* with the imposing relationship
between colonnade and figures (a juxtaposition which was to
be a favourite with painters until the time of Rubens and
beyond), arranged in the same way as in the *Fire in Borgo,*
introduces a strong representational technique. The composition of the *Death of Ananias* is even more impressive,
with its iconographic echoes of the *School of Athens* and
the *Expulsion of Heliodorus;* the way the two groups revolve is brilliantly original, and so is the contrast between
the static hieratic figure in the centre and the twisted motion of the two figures in the foreground. The two masterpieces of this series are *The Draught of Fishes* and
Christ's Charge to Peter (see p. 25).

The Draught of Fishes is set in a scene of utter tranquillity,
beside a lake; from the distance comes a flight of birds, some
of them landing on the strand, in the right, giving definition
to the perspective of the landscape. The strand curves round
two circular groups of figures, which are separated by the
standing figure of the saint. The right hand group of figures
is full of dramatic tension, but this is dissipated in the
elongated forms of the two apostles, stretched in supplication
towards Christ. Christ himself, with a gesture, stills the
turbulence of the drama and leads the eye on into the
peaceful landscape over which herons fly.

The composition of *Christ's Charge to Peter* is if anything
more lyrical and sublime; it is clearly derived from Masaccio's *Tribute,* and as a homage to the earlier master
shows a strong sense of history. It bears the unmistakable
imprint of Raphael's imagination. In a broad landscape, as
pure and transparent as the landscape in the *Dispute,* the
figures are disposed according to a plan which is perfection
in itself. Whether Raphael was entirely responsible for it
is immaterial. The wonderfully straightforward, monumental design flows so smoothly and so harmoniously from the
figure of Christ, that this is surely one of the greatest of

Christ's Charge to Peter, tapestry cartoon. London, Victoria and Albert Museum

human achievements, a milestone in human experience. In one of his last works Raphael has truly achieved his ideal: a perfectly symmetrical design realised with the utmost poetry. The most interesting examples of Raphael's increasing involvement with architecture are really to be found in his paintings. Even the limpid plan of a chapel, such as the Chigi Chapel in Santa Maria del Popolo, which gives such dynamic expression to the ideas of Bramante, does not achieve the same heights as the imagined settings of the *Dispute* or *Christ's Charge to Peter*.

Raphael had by now risen, although he was still a young man, to a position of vital importance in the world of art. In his next painting, the *Transfiguration* (*pls 74-5*), he introduces an even more complex narrative scheme: the triumph of Christ is organized on a ground plan very like the one used in the early *Marriage of the Virgin* in the Brera. The importance of this painting is greatly increased if one remembers that Raphael, in order to confound the critics at the Papal Court who were accusing him of exploiting his pupils' work, had decided to paint the *Transfiguration* entirely by himself. The composition is extremely daring: the central plane revealed by the cleft in the rock on which the apostles are lying, opens out into a great spiral culminating in the symbolic sphere containing the vision; this is linked with the foreground group by a triangle of convergent perspectives. The symbolic and structural complexity of the painting (recently the subject of a detailed study) is obscured by the dramatic intensity of the figure of Christ, an echo of the 'vision' theme first introduced in the *Sistine Madonna*.

The painting was interrupted by the death of Raphael, and as a result is chiefly the work of pupils working without their master's guidance. During the regal funeral accorded to Raphael by the Papal Court, this painting, half-finished but dazzling, was displayed at one end of the catafalque.

Raphael and the critics

Critical attitudes to Raphael, his works and his theories constitute one of the most complex chapters in the history of art. During his lifetime his activity was acknowledged throughout the arts and literature, even more so perhaps than the activity of Michelangelo. However, after his death this situation changed appreciably. His biggest rival, Michelangelo, lived on for many years, and Vasari's *Lives of the Painters*, which was widely accepted as an official text, placed Michelangelo at the top of the artistic tree, so that Raphael's stock went down. He received effective support from Dolce's *Dialogo della Pittura*, published in Venice in 1557, and from the favourable judgements of Aretino and Castiglione. His status was not enhanced by the work of his pupils, in particular Giulio Romano, who very quickly became violently manneristic. They finally adopted painting techniques which were directly derived from Michelangelo, and not, as Dolce had predicted, from the purism and classicism of Raphael. A strong stimulus to the re-instatement of Raphael in the painters' Parnassus was provided by the Bolognese Accademia in the seventeenth century, and later by the Roman Accademia. These academies looked to Raphael as one of their safest strongholds against the invasion of the baroque; and it was they that gave birth to the ' classical ideal ' typical of the seventeenth century. This ' classical ideal ' was to be a point of departure for theorists such as Bellori, and also for painters, including Poussin (though he had reservations about Raphael) and Claude Lorrain.

These attitudes towards Raphael remained constant in painting, particularly in the Bolognese and Roman schools, throughout the seventeenth century, and in the eighteenth century they became one of the fundamental components of so-called neoclassicism. Appeals to the example of Raphael are to be found in the works of writers and artists such as Winckelmann, Albarotti, Mengs and Reynolds, culminating in the praises of Goethe.

The coming of romanticism naturally brought about a sudden reversal of opinion on the part of artists and critics. The careful thought and measurement which is an integral part of Raphael's work conflicted with the romantic search for spontaneity which led to the rediscovery of the Italian primitive painters. Raphael's youthful works, in which the premeditation is least obvious, remained in favour.

Nevertheless it is interesting to note that the study of Raphael was fundamental to the art of that supreme painter, Ingres; and one of the greatest romantic painters, Delacroix, noted some extremely acute critical judgements of Raphael in his diary. The judgements of scholars such as Passavant, Bianchini, Burckhardt and Morelli show far less insight. We must look forward to the intervention of Cavalcaselle (*Rafaello, la sua vita e le sue opere*, Florence 1882-5, with J. Crowe) for the earliest critical monograph on Raphael. Notable among later studies are the monograph of Rosemberg and Gronau (Leipzig 1909); *Raphael* by A. Venturi (Urbino 1920, reprinted several times); monographs by Suida (Oxford 1941), and Gamba (Paris 1932); Ortolani's classic work (Bergamo 1942); Fischel's monograph (London 1948) and Ragghianti's study of the *Baglioni Deposition* (Milan 1949). More recent studies have been contributed by Camesasca, Schoene, Bettini, Mellini and Brizio.

Notes on the Plates

1 Resurrection. Oil on canvas, 52 × 44 cm. São Paolo, Brazil, Museu de Arte. Itemized in 1857 by Bode in the Kinnaird collection, it was attributed to various hands. Berenson assigned it to the school of Perugino. Regteren von Altena in 1927 showed convincingly that the *Resurrection* was the work of the young Raphael. In 1955 Ragghianti pronounced it to be one of his earliest works, with the *Baglioni Annunciation* in Perugia. Longhi also accepts this attribution, pointing out that the canvas is typical of the young painter's Pinturicchio phase. It was taken to Brazil after the Second World War.

2 Coronation of the Virgin. Oil on wooden panel, transferred to canvas. 267 × 163 cm. Rome, Pinacoteca Vaticana. Commissioned by Maddalena degli Oddi in 1502 for the family chapel in the church of San Francesco in Perugia. Requisitioned by the French in 1797, it was taken to France where, because of damage to the panel, it was transferred to canvas. It was returned to Italy in 1815 and went to the Vatican, where it is today. When it was transferred from wood to canvas it was joined to form an altarpiece with the predella showing the *Annunciation*, the *Presentation at the Temple* and the *Epiphany*. The dating, derived from documents of the period, has been confirmed as 1502 or 1503 by Fischel, Ragghianti, Brizio, Camesasca, Berenson, Suida and Carli, the last four regarding 1503 as the probable year in which it was painted.

3 St Sebastian. Oil on panel, 43 × 34 cm. Bergamo, Accademia Carrara. In the past it belonged to the Zurla di Crema collection, the collection of Giuseppe Longhi and the Lochis collection. Its attribution to Raphael is undisputed. It has been dated 1501-2 by Ortolani, Fischel, Gamba, Longhi, Camesasca, Brizio, and 1503 by Venturi, Ottino della Chiesa and Gronau. It was certainly painted before 1504; its exact date is difficult to establish, though the scale of the modelling suggests the years 1502-3, when Raphael's relationship with Perugino was at its closest.

4-5 Marriage of the Virgin. Oil on curved panel. 170 × 117 cm. Milan, Pinacoteca di Brera. Signed and dated on the frieze and spandrels of the temple colonnade: RAPHAEL URBINAS MDIII. Commissioned by the Albizzini family for the Chapel of St Joseph in the church of San Francesco in Città di Castello, where it remained until it was given to the Napoleonic General Lechi by the municipality; Lechi soon sold it back to the Milanese merchant Sannazzari. In 1804 it was inherited by the Ospedale Maggiore, Milan, and in 1806 acquired by the Accademia di Brera. It was imperfectly restored at the end of the nineteenth century, and was recently slashed by a lunatic. Brilliant restoration has completely concealed the damage.

6 Ansidei Madonna (Madonna enthroned with St John and St Nicholas). London, National Gallery. Oil on panel, 274 × 152 cm. Begun in Perugia in about 1504 and finished in 1506 for the Ansidei Chapel in San Lorenzo dei Serviti. It was acquired in 1764 by Lord Spencer, and a copy by Nicola Monti put in its place. Having come into the possession of the Duke of Marlborough, it was acquired in 1885 by the National Gallery. The panel is dated illegibly on the hem of the drape, below the left hand of the Virgin. The date is variously interpreted as xdv (Passavant and Waagen) or mdvi (Cavalcaselle). Cavalcaselle's date seems more probable and coincides with his theory that the painting was executed at two different periods. This theory has been accepted by Longhi and by most scholars. The only part of the predella which has survived is the *Preaching of St John to the multitude*, in the Mersey collection, London.

7 Vision of a Knight. Oil on panel, 17 × 17 cm. London, National Gallery. This and the *Three Graces*, now at Chantilly, belonged to the Borghese collection, Rome. At the end of the eighteenth century it was transferred to England, to the Ottley collection. After belonging to three private owners it was acquired by the National Gallery. The allegorical meaning of the painting has been variously interpreted. The most plausible solution in my opinion is that proposed by Chastel, who sees this as a reference to Cicero's *Somnium Scipionis*, ' The Dream of Scipio ', a myth which was very popular with the neo-Platonists. The work shows Scipio faced with a choice between Pallas, symbol of moral greatness, and Venus, symbol of glory and worldly pleasure. The small panel of the *Three Graces* probably shows the apple of the Hesperides given by the Graces to the conquering hero. The fact that the measurements of this panel are identical with those of the *Vision of a Knight* make Panofsky's theory that the two formed a diptych very plausible. Cavalcaselle first dated the work 1504, immediately before Raphael's move to Florence. This date was moved forward by later scholars, who regard this panel and its twin, the *Three Graces*, as one of Raphael's first works. The most accurate dating is probably that put forward more recently by Longhi, Ragghianti, Camesasca, Brizio, Chastel and others, who all regard this as a mature work of the artist's Florentine period (1505).

8 St George. Florence, Uffizi, Gabinetto dei Disegni e delle Stampe, no. 430 E. Study for the *St George* in the Louvre (*pl. 9*). Another study for this painting is no. 429 E in the same collection.

9 St George and the Dragon. Oil on panel, 31 × 27 cm. Paris, Louvre. This and the *St Michael*, also in the Louvre, were part of the collection of Charles I of England, sold to Cardinal Mazarin. The Cardinal's heirs sold it to Louis XIV. It is datable to the early years of Raphael's Florentine period, according to most scholars. It might have been part of a diptych with the *St Michael* (which has the same measurements); but this is more difficult to establish. Certain art historians contradict this theory by pointing out that the *St Michael* is stylistically inferior and was probably painted before Raphael left Urbino for Tuscany.

10   Madonna and Child. Pencil. Florence, Uffizi, Gabinetto dei Disegni e delle Stampe, no. RZ III 105. This is the first circular drawing for the *Madonna of the Grand Duke.*

11   Madonna of the Grand Duke. Florence, Pitti. Oil on panel, 84 × 55 cm. It once belonged to the painter Carlo Dolci. In 1799 it was bought by Ferdinand III, Grand Duke of Hapsburg-Lorraine, who admired it so tremendously that he refused to be separated from it even when he went on long journeys. The traditional date given to it and accepted by most critics is 1505; Longhi attributes it to the year before Raphael's arrival in Florence. Camesasca, by searching behind numerous re-paintings to the somewhat disfigured background, supports a later date (1506-7).

12   Christ giving his benediction. Oil on panel, 30 × 25 cm. Brescia, Pinacoteca Tosio Martinengo. This used to belong to the Mosca di Pesaro collection. It was transferred to the Tosio collection in 1832. The dating of the painting is controversial. Fischel, Gronau, Venturi and Ortolani attribute it to Raphael's Umbrian period. Cavalcaselle suggested 1504 as a more plausible date. The structure of the figure of Christ is clearly linked to Raphael's seeing Leonardo's *Leda* in Florence in 1504.

13   Tempi Madonna. Oil on panel, 77 × 53 cm. Munich, Alte Pinakothek. Mentioned by Cinelli as being in the house of the Tempi family, it was bought by Ludwig of Bavaria in 1829. Its date is somewhere between 1506 and 1508. 1508 (supported by Ortolani, Carli and Longhi) is the more likely date, in view of the structural relationship between this painting and *St Catherine of Alexandria*, and with the central group of the *Foligno Madonna*; it anticipates the style of the *Madonna of the Chair.*

14   La Belle Jardinière. Oil on panel, 122 × 80 cm. Paris, Louvre. Signed RAPHAELLO URB. and dated MDVII. Identified as the work undertaken for Filippo Sergardi, left unfinished by Raphael and completed by Rodolfo del Ghirlandaio, mentioned by Vasari. It seems to have been acquired by Francis I of France directly from Sergardi in Siena.

15   Madonna of the Goldfinch. Oil on panel, 107 × 77 cm. Florence, Uffizi. According to Vasari it was painted for Vincenzo Nasi. It was badly damaged by the collapse of the Nasi house in 1547 and was restored by Michele di Ridolfo del Ghirlandaio. From 1666 it belonged to the collection of Cardinal Carlo de' Medici in the Uffizi. It is unanimously dated 1506 by art historians.

16-17 Canigiani Madonna (Madonna with St John and St Elizabeth). Oil on panel, 132 × 98 cm. Munich, Alte Pinakothek. Signed RAPHAEL URBINAS. Painted for Domenico Canigiani, it was in his house (where Vasari saw it) until, at an unknown date, it passed into the Medici collection, where it was first recorded in the early years of the seventeenth century. Anna Maria Luisa, daughter of the Grand Duke Cosimo, presented it to her husband William, Elector Palatine. It was taken to Düsseldorf to the Elector's collection and then taken to Munich in 1801 to escape the clutches of Napoleon's armies. It is unanimously dated 1507. A copy in the Corsini Gallery shows a flight of angels in the background. This detail, plus the poor state of preservation and the numerous repaintings of the sky in the Munich version, suggest that Reber is correct in conjecturing that there were angels in the original painting which have now been removed or covered up.

18 Baglioni Deposition. Oil on panel, 184 × 176 cm. Rome, Galleria Borghese. Signed and dated: RAPHAEL URBINAS MDVII. Commissioned by Atalanta Baglioni to commemorate her son Grifonetto, killed by a relative to avenge the death of four other kinsmen whom Grifonetto himself had murdered. It was hung in the Baglioni Chapel in San Francesco al Prato, Perugia, where it remained until 1608. In 1608 it was sent by the friars of San Francesco to Pope Paul V, who gave it to his nephew, Cardinal Scipione Borghese. To placate the indignant citizens of Perugia a copy was made by the Cavalier d'Arpino. This was looted by the French in 1787 and returned in 1813. There are many extant studies for the work which demonstrate how elaborate a composition it is; these drawings are perhaps the most complete and coherent guide to Raphael as a draughtsman. The hand of an assistant can be detected in parts of the painting, possibly that of Alfani (Cavalcaselle, Ragghianti).

19 Study for the Baglioni Deposition. Pencil drawing, 182 × 205 cm. Oxford, Ashmolean Museum. First plan for the *Baglioni Deposition* (*pl. 18*), it is still on a traditional framework reminiscent of Perugino, with iconographic details from Fra' Bartolomeo.

20-1 Studies for the Baglioni Deposition. Pen and ink drawings. London, British Museum. no. 1895/9/15/616-7. Final sketch for the swooning figure of Mary in the *Deposition* (*pl. 18*). Through a study of the skeleton Raphael builds up the final composition of the figure.

22-3 Study for the Baglioni Deposition. Pen and ink drawing. London, British Museum, no. 1855/2/149. The first study of the painting as a whole.

24 The Dumb Girl. Oil on panel, 64 × 48 cm. Urbino, Galleria Nazionale delle Marche. This used to belong to the Uffizi, but was transferred to Urbino in 1927. Its attribution to Raphael is extremely controversial. It is denied by, among others, Rumohr, Cavalcaselle, Morelli, Rosemberg and Freedberg, and supported by Venturi, Serra,

Locchi, Modigliani, Gamba, Camesasca and Brizio. Its date is probably 1506-7, judging by its construction, which places it above even the finest portions of the Doni portraits.

25 Portrait of a Lady with a Unicorn. Oil on panel, 65 × 51 cm. Rome, Galleria Borghese. This appears in the Borghese Inventory of 1760 as the work of Perugino. It was certainly repainted by a Florentine painter, at the middle of the sixteenth century, after the lower part of the work had been damaged. During the repainting the unicorn was painted out and a spiked wheel placed in the hands of the model so that it was transformed into a portrait of St Catherine of Alexandria. It was then attributed to Ridolfo del Ghirlandaio; later to Granacci and Andrea del Sarto. In 1928 Longhi attributed it to Raphael, and in the same year the over-painting was removed and the work restored to its original state. It was subsequently accepted by most scholars (excepting recently Freedberg) as dating from 1505-6.

26-7 Madonna of the Baldachin. Oil on panel, 276 × 224 cm. Florence, Pitti. Painted for the Dei Chapel in Santo Spirito, and left unfinished by Raphael when he departed for Rome. Prince Ferdinando de' Medici acquired it in 1697 from the Pieve di Pescia, where it had hung since the sixteenth century at least. Ferdinando gave it to Niccolò and Agostino Cassana, who finished it, adding the horizontal strip at the top, above the canopy, to enlarge it to the same dimensions as a picture it was to hang beside. It was commandeered by Napoleon in 1799 and returned in 1815. The structure of this masterpiece was the basis for a series of contemporary works by painters such as Fra' Bartolomeo, Andrea del Sarto and Pontormo. As an example it was very influential in the compositions of painters such as Lorenzo Lotto; the theory that certain details reminiscent of Venetian painting stem from Raphael's contact with Fra' Bartolomeo (who had lived for some time in Venice) has been discounted.

28 Portrait of Agnolo Doni. Oil on panel, 63 × 45 cm. Florence, Pitti. This and the portrait of Doni's wife (*pl. 29*) remained in the Doni collection in Florence until 1826. Then it passed into the collection of Leopold II of Tuscany. It can be dated accurately to 1506. According to a theory of Venturi, supported by Marangoni and accepted almost universally by critics, this portrait was painted immediately before the portrait of Maddalena. On the back of the panel there is a monochrome painting of the myth of Deucalion and Pyrrha and the Flood, painted by a late follower of Raphael.

29 Portrait of Maddalena Doni. Oil on panel, 63 × 45 cm. Florence, Pitti. Apart from the unsupported opinion of Ortolani, who thinks this is a portrait of Doni's sister-in-law, this is generally regarded as a likeness of Maddalena Strozzi, married to Agnolo Doni in 1503. On the back of the panel is another monochrome painting by the same hand as the one on the other portrait, showing Deucalion and Pyrrha being saved from the flood.

30-3 Dispute over the Holy Sacrament. Fresco in a lunette, base measurement 770 cm. Rome, Stanze Vaticane. This was the first of the frescoes to be painted in the so-called Stanza della Segnatura. This chamber was originally part of Julius II's private apartments, and it contained the Papal library. The name was given later, when the Ecclesiastical Tribunal sat in the chamber. The title given to this particular fresco is based on a questionable seventeenth-century interpretation of a passage from Vasari's *Lives*: the subject is really the *Exaltation of the Eucharist*. The opinion that this was the first of the frescoes to be painted in the chamber is currently accepted, and this means that the date of the painting is 1508-9. It was nearly all painted by Raphael himself: only the figure presumed to be Francesco Maria della Rovere, the Pope's nephew (fourth on the left in the foreground, the figure pointing to the altar) is less well executed and has been attributed by some critics to Sodoma (see also p. 16).

34-6 The School of Athens. Fresco in a lunette, base measurement 770 cm. Rome, Stanze Vaticane. Painted in 1509-10, immediately after the *Dispute*. it represents Truth in its rational aspect; in the *Dispute*, Revealed Truth is represented. In this painting can be found portraits of the greatest philosophers of the ancient world, each indicated by a personal symbol. Plato (on the left) and Aristotle are the central figures. The fresco is one of the most complete plans of Florentine neo-Platonism as it was adopted at the Papal Court. The inclusion of representatives of the figurative arts (Leonardo, Michelangelo and Raphael himself) in the ranks of the sages is not really intended (as has been often said) to show the victory of painting over the theories of neo-Platonism (after Plato's original condemnation of the arts, the neo-Platonists had re-instated only the art of poetry). Raphael wanted to show the ideological and philosophical potential of painting itself. According to some critics the figure of Heraclitus, sitting in the centre foreground (leaning against the rock) is probably a portrait of Michelangelo, added to the painting after Raphael had seen the finished ceiling of the Sistine Chapel (1510).

37 Group of Philosophers. Silverpoint on grey paper, highlighted with white lead. Vienna, Albertina. Study for the left hand group, with Pythagoras, for *The School of Athens*.

38-40 Parnassus. Fresco in a lunette, base measurement 670 cm. Rome, Stanze Vaticane. Dated in the window JULIUS II LIGUR. PONT. MAX. ANN. CHRIST. MDXI. PONTIFICAT. SUI. VIII. The fresco represents Beauty, under the aspect of Poetry. The date 1511 probably refers to the conclusion of the whole chamber, that is to the completion of the painting of the *Virtues* on the front wall. This fresco can be dated to the years 1509-10. The state of preservation is unsatisfactory in many places, particularly around the sky where overpainting is visible (see also p. 16).

41-3 Expulsion of Heliodorus from the Temple. Fresco in a lunette, base measurement 750 cm. Rome, Stanze Vaticane. This work gave its name to the third chamber in order of execution, the Stanza di Eliodoro. In each fresco an episode showing the direct intervention of God in political and popular life is portrayed. A reference to Julius II's politico-religious programme is clearly intended. The fresco shows Heliodorus who, having despoiled the temple in Jerusalem, is hurled to the ground and punished for sacrilege. In the background the high priest Onias is praying. On the left is a portrait of Julius II being borne aloft by a group of people (see text p. 19). Most critics, in agreement with Cavalcaselle, consider this to be the earliest fresco in the chamber, consigning it to 1511-12. The work of pupils is easy to detect; the group of Heliodorus and the horseman is probably the work of Giulio Romano, the women on the left, of Giovanni da Udine. It was restored in the seventeenth century by Maratta.

44   Leo I forcing Attila to a halt. Fresco in a lunette, base measurement 750 cm. Rome, Stanze Vaticane. This fresco was painted on a wall which had previously been decorated with a series of *condottieri* by Bramante. The subject of the work is the famous encounter between Attila the Hun and Pope Leo I on the Mincio in 452. Raphael portrays the event as happening in the environs of Rome. During the execution of the fresco (1513-14) Julius II died. For this reason the face of Leo I does not bear any resemblance to the Della Rovere pope: it shows Leo X de' Medici, the newly elected pope. The subject seems to allude in some way to the battle of Ravenna (11 April 1512) in which the French were expelled from Italy. The painting was almost entirely carried out by apprentices. Longhi avers that the background landscape is by Lotto.

45-7   The Mass of Bolsena. Fresco in a lunette, base measurement 660 cm. Rome, Stanze Vaticane. The division of the window bears the inscription JULIUS II LIGUR PONT MAX ANN CHRIST MDXII PONTIFICAT SUI VIII. This fresco was painted on a wall which had previously been decorated by Bramantino with portraits of *condottieri*. The subject is an event which took place in 1263: a Bohemian priest, saying mass over the tomb of St Christina in Bolsena, experienced doubts about the truth of the mistery of transubstantiation and was reassured by seeing drops of blood dripping from the consecrated host. This miracle gave rise to the festival of Corpus Domini, instituted by a bull of Pope Urban IV (1264). The work of pupils can be found only in the group of women on the left; according to Longhi and Zampetti the group of seated figures was painted by Lorenzo Lotto.

48-51   Liberation of St Peter. Fresco in a lunette, base measurement 660 cm. Rome, Stanze Vaticane. An inscription on the architrave of the window bears the date: LEO X PONT MAX ANN CHRIST MDXIIII PONTIFICAT SUI II. Painted over an earlier fresco by Piero della Francesca. It represents the story, from the Acts of the Apostles, according to which St Peter, imprisoned in Jerusalem, was freed by an angel who appeared to him in a dream. When he awoke the saint found himself out of prison. The date of the painting has been much debated by scholars, but to my mind the date in the inscription on the architrave of the window (1509) does not conflict with stylistic evidence. The hand of pupils, and in particular Giulio Romano, can be seen in the thick colouring of parts of the work, but does not seem so obvious as in other frescoes in the same chamber.

52-3 Portrait of Leo X between two cardinals. Oil on panel, 154 × 119 cm. Florence, Uffizi. The two cardinals are Giulio de' Medici and Luigi de' Rossi. In 1589 the painting was in the Uffizi. From 1799 to 1815 it was in Paris with the other spoils of Napoleon. The origin of Andrea del Sarto's copy, now in Naples, is famous. Vasari narrates that Federigo II, Lord of Mantua, saw the picture in the house of Ottaviano de' Medici in Florence, and wrote to Clement VII asking to be given the work. The Pope ordered Ottaviano to send the painting to Mantua, but the Grand Duke asked for time to have a copy made for himself; then he ordered Andrea del Sarto to make a copy and sent the copy to Gonzaga, and not the original. The date of the work is known (apart from stylistic considerations), because of an external event. De' Rossi is shown here in cardinal's robes; he was made a cardinal in 1517 and died in 1519; therefore the work must have been painted between those years.

54-5 Foligno Madonna. Oil on panel, transferred to canvas, 320 × 194 cm. Rome, Pinacoteca Vaticana. Commissioned by Sigismondo de' Conti (shown kneeling at the bottom), as a thank-offering when his house remained unscathed after being struck by lightning. Hung in the Aracoeli, it was transported in 1565 to the church of Sant'Anna in Foligno. In 1797 it was taken to Paris where it was transferred to canvas. Apart from Venturi, who proposed 1509 as its date, it is universally dated 1511-12. The unusual narrative detail in the background (the episode of the house spared by a thunderbolt) is attributed by Cavalcaselle to Battista Dossi, and by Longhi to Dosso Dossi himself. This opinion, shared by many scholars, is in fact difficult to establish with certainty.

56 Sistine Madonna. Oil on canvas, 265 × 196 cm. Dresden, Gemäldegalerie. Painted for the monks of the church of San Sisto in Piacenza, it was sold to Augustus III, Elector of Saxony, in 1754. In its place a copy by Nogari was hung. After the Second World War it was taken to Moscow and later returned to Dresden. The fact that it is painted on canvas, unusual for Raphael, has given rise to various hypotheses, the most plausible of which is that it was painted for use as a processional banner. Art historians have assigned various dates to this painting, between 1513 and 1516; the later date is supported by Venturi, Gamba, Golzio, Ragghianti and Camesasca and seems the most likely, judging by the structure and proportions of the painting.

57 Madonna of the Chair. Oil on a circular panel, diameter 71 cm. Florence, Pitti. Soon after Raphael's death this was in the

Medici collection in the Uffizi. In the first decade of the seventeenth century it was transferred to the Pitti. It was commandeered by the French in 1799 and restored in 1815. Most scholars date it around 1515-16, soon after the *Madonna of the Fish*. Part of the structure of the work can be found, with variations, in the *Madonna of the Tent* in the Alte Pinakothek, Munich, which was probably painted immediately before this.

58-9 Triumph of Galatea. Fresco, 295 × 225 cm. Rome, Farnesina, Sala della Galatea. Commissioned by Prince Chigi when a previous commission to Sebastiano del Piombo failed to meet with his approval. The date of execution has been controversial but a record by Gallo (*De viridario Augustini Chigi etc...*) in 1511 mentions the fresco, which settles the question. The hand of Giulio Romano is obvious, even if not quite as drastically so as Cavalcaselle made it seem. The subject is taken from Theocritus and Ovid, perhaps via Politian's *Giostra*, and represents Palemon as a boy, riding on a dolphin, leading the triumphal procession of Galatea.

60 Isaiah. Fresco, 250 × 155 cm. Rome, church of Sant'Agostino. Commissioned by Giovanni Goritz, apostolic protonotary from Luxembourg, whose name appears in the Greek dedication to St Anne and the Virgin Mary written on the placard at the top. Vasari narrates that the fresco was painted immediately after Raphael had felt the overwhelming impact of the unveiling of the first cycle of the ceiling of the Sistine Chapel in 1510. Critics are almost unanimous in dating *Isaiah* 1511-12. A further proof of this is the copy ordered by Julius II of the two *putti* on either side, one of which is now in the Accademia di San Luca; as Julius II died in 1513 the fresco cannot have been painted after that date.

61 Portrait of a Cardinal. Oil on panel, 79 × 62 cm. Madrid, Prado. There have been many attempts to identify this likeness with famous prelates at the Papal Court, but these have led nowhere. The date of this masterpiece of sixteenth-century portraiture was suggested by Rosemberg as 1518, but this would make it too late for the inclusion of the very obvious Florentine details which can be found in it. A more probable date would be 1510-11, making it contemporaneous with the beginning of the decorations in the Stanza della Segnatura.

62-5 Fire in Borgo. Fresco in a lunette, base measurement 670 cm. Rome, Stanze Vaticane. The fresco gave its name to the first chamber of the apartments of Julius II, the Stanza dell'Incendio. Chronologically, this one was painted third, between the years 1514 and 1517. The subjects chosen to decorate the chamber seem to continue the political theme of the Stanza di Eliodoro. But in order to gratify the new Pope Leo X each episode contains a reference to a pope with the name Leo. The invention of each episode seems to have some connection with Castiglione. Besides this picture, the other frescoes in this chamber are of the *Battle of Ostia*, the *Coro-*

nation of Charlemagne and the *Justification of Leo III.* Raphael's contribution to them was virtually nil. The four paintings in the vault are by Perugino. The theme of *Fire in Borgo* is from the *Liber Pontificalis*, and tells how Leo IV miraculously extinguished a fire which broke out in the crowded quarter of Borgo. In keeping with Leo X's campaign to revive the classical history of Rome, Raphael includes mythical personages and events in the story, portraying in effect the Burning of Troy. The work of his pupils, which can be found throughout, does not detract from the exceptional structure of the painting, nor from its seminal importance to sixteenth-century painting. The group on the left reveals the handiwork of Giulio Romano, as does the right-hand group, including the famous water-carrier. Penni was apparently responsible for the centre of the painting.

66-7 St Cecilia. Oil on panel, transferred to canvas, 220 × 136 cm. Bologna, Pinacoteca Nazionale. Commissioned by Elena, wife of Benedetto dall'Olio, for the church of San Giovanni in Monte, Bologna, in 1514. Vasari says that the commission was given to Raphael by Cardinal Antonio Pucci. Commandeered by the French in 1798, it was transferred to canvas. In 1815 it was returned to Bologna. According to Vasari the musical instruments were painted by Giovanni da Udine; the hand of Giulio Romano can be seen clearly in the layout of the painting. The dates advanced for it waver between 1515 and 1518. It was probably painted soon after it had been ordered, that is in 1514-15. This is supported, as Longhi points out, by the echoes of it which are to be found in Emilian paintings from that date onwards.

68 Vision of Ezekiel. Oil on panel, 40 × 30 cm. Florence, Pitti. This was in the Uffizi at least from 1589. From 1799 to 1815 it was in France, among the spoils of Napoleon. Vasari maintains that it was painted for Count Ercolani di Bologna, in whose house he claims to have seen it. Most art historians place it between the years 1516-18, with a preference for the latter date. The participation of Giulio Romano is disputed; according to some he was completely responsible for painting the picture, and if so he achieved an exceptionally high standard both technically and artistically.

69 Portrait of Fedra Inghirami. Oil on panel, 90 × 62 cm. Florence, Pitti. A complicated problem is raised by the existence of a brilliant copy in Boston which came directly from the Palazzo Inghirami in Volterra. The version shown here came to the Pitti from the collection of Cardinal Leopoldo de' Medici. It was taken by the French in 1799 and returned to the Pitti in 1815. In the course of a heated critical controversy (Carli, Francini, Ciaranfi, Marangoni, Camesasca, *et al.*) few scholars seem to entertain the obvious hypothesis that as both pictures are so fine they must both be original. This suggestion might be supported by the fact that, according to Vasari, Leo X ordered a portrait of the Cardinal, his close friend and colleague; this work, which remained in the possession of the Medici, is obviously the one now in Florence. The copy which was in the Palazzo Inghirami and is now in Boston could have been painted for the cardinal himself, as he would have wanted to own such a fine portrait of himself. Both are impeccable; in the American version a finer treatment of the coloured robe could be due to its better state of preservation. The agreed date of execution is 1514-15.

70 Study for the Madonna of the Fish. Red chalk on paper. Florence, Uffizi, Gabinetto dei Disegni e delle Stampe, no. RZ VIII 371. This was the final study for the painting now in Madrid (*pl. 71*).

71 Madonna of the Fish. Oil on panel, transferred to canvas, 215 × 158 cm. Madrid, Prado. It is known as the *Madonna of the Fish* because of the symbol held by Tobias on the left. It was probably painted for the Chapel of Giovanbattista del Duco in the church of San Domenico, Naples, where it could be found in 1524. In 1638 it was acquired by the Spanish Viceroy, the Duke of Medina, and two years later was sent to Madrid. Carried off by the French, it was transferred to canvas in Paris in 1813. It was returned to Spain in 1822. It is certain that pupils helped with the painting, including Giulio Romano. The figures on the left are usually attributed to him. It was probably painted in about 1513-1514, at the same time as the *Madonna dell'Impannata*.

72 Lady with a Veil. Oil on panel, 85 × 64 cm. Florence, Pitti. This was seen soon after the death of Raphael in the house of the Botti family in Florence, but in 1619 passed into the Medici family. It was thought for a long time to be a portrait of La Fornarina. The likeness is that of the model painted in the *Sistine Madonna*. The structure of the upper part is directly linked to the Dresden canvas in fact. Certain scholars have denied that this is by Raphael (Burckhardt, Bode, Muntz). Its date is close to that of the *Sistine Madonna*, not only because the same model appears in both, but also because of great similarity in use of colour and technique.

73 Holy Family of Francis I. Oil on panel, transferred to canvas, 207 × 140 cm. Paris, Louvre. Signed and dated RAPHAEL URBINAS PINGEBAT MDXVIII. Commissioned with the *St Michael* (also in the Louvre) by Lorenzo de' Medici as a gift from Leo X to the King of France. It was delivered to Fontainebleau in June 1519, and immediately acquired a fame that was legendary. It was transferred to Versailles a few years later, having been somewhat damaged, and in about 1540 was restored by Primaticcio. In 1753 it was transferred to canvas. The intervention of Giulio Romano has been admitted since Vasari's time; his part in it was great, although the complex composition is one of the most notable spatial structures of Raphael's last years.

74-5 Transfiguration. Oil on panel, 405 × 278 cm. Rome, Pinacoteca Vaticana. The career of this painting is very well-known. It was commissioned by Cardinal Giulio de' Medici to be sent to Narbonne

Cathedral. Another altar in the same church had been allotted to Sebastiano del Piombo who, apparently, either from jealousy or because he misunderstood Raphael's refusal to paint anything without assistance (a refusal which would have been incomprehensible to any educated Venetian painter), had originated the widespread criticism of Raphael at the Papal Court for relying on pupils too much. It seems that Raphael consequently undertook to paint this work entirely by himself. But he died while he was engaged on it. The upper part was nearly finished, but the lower part was only sketched in. It was finished by Giulio Romano and Penni and hung in San Pietro in Montorio in 1523. It was carried off by the French in 1797 and given an unnecessary cleaning. In 1815 it was restored to the Vatican, where it still is.

76 Annunciation. Pen and wash drawing. Paris, Louvre, Cabinet des Dessins, no. 3860. Study for part of the *Coronation of the Virgin* now in the Vatican.

77 St Catherine of Alexandria. Pencil drawing. Paris, Louvre, Cabinet des Dessins, no. 3871. Study for the painting in the National Gallery, London, unanimously dated 1506-7.

78 Madonna and Child with St John. Pen drawing. Florence, Uffizi, Gabinetto dei Disegni e delle Stampe, no. F III 126. Study for the *Esterhazy Madonna*, now in Budapest (*c.* 1506).

79 Sketches for a Madonna and Child. Pen drawing. London, British Museum, vol. 64.L.36. This dates from the latter years of Raphael's residence in Florence.

1

3

4

5

SALVE·MATER·CHRISTI

6

7

8

9

13

15

16

17

18

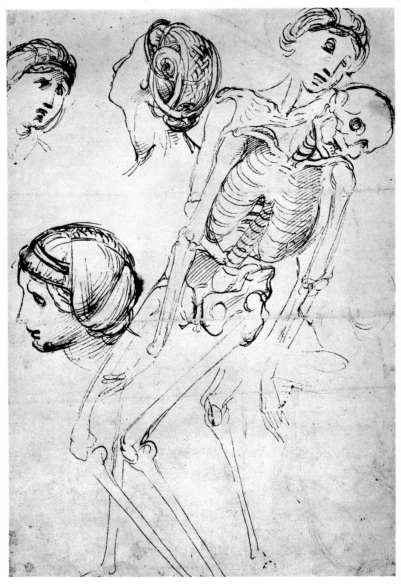

21

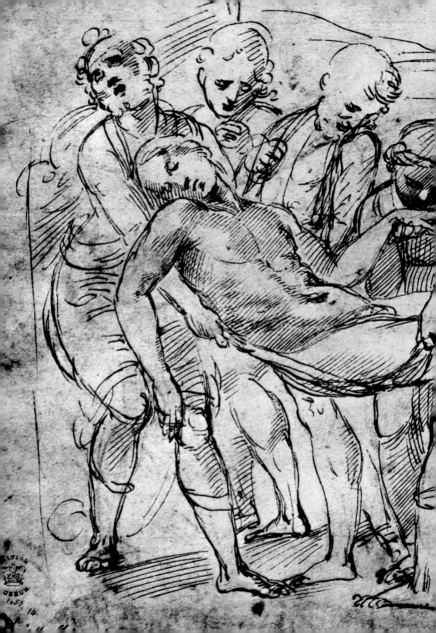

25

28

31

33

37

X · ANN · D · M · D · X · IIII

47

55

ΠΑΡΘΕΝΙΚΗ ΘΕΟΤΟΚΟ
Κ ΛΥΤΡΩΤΗ ΧΡΙΣΤΟ
· ΙΩ · ΚΟΡ

60

61

64

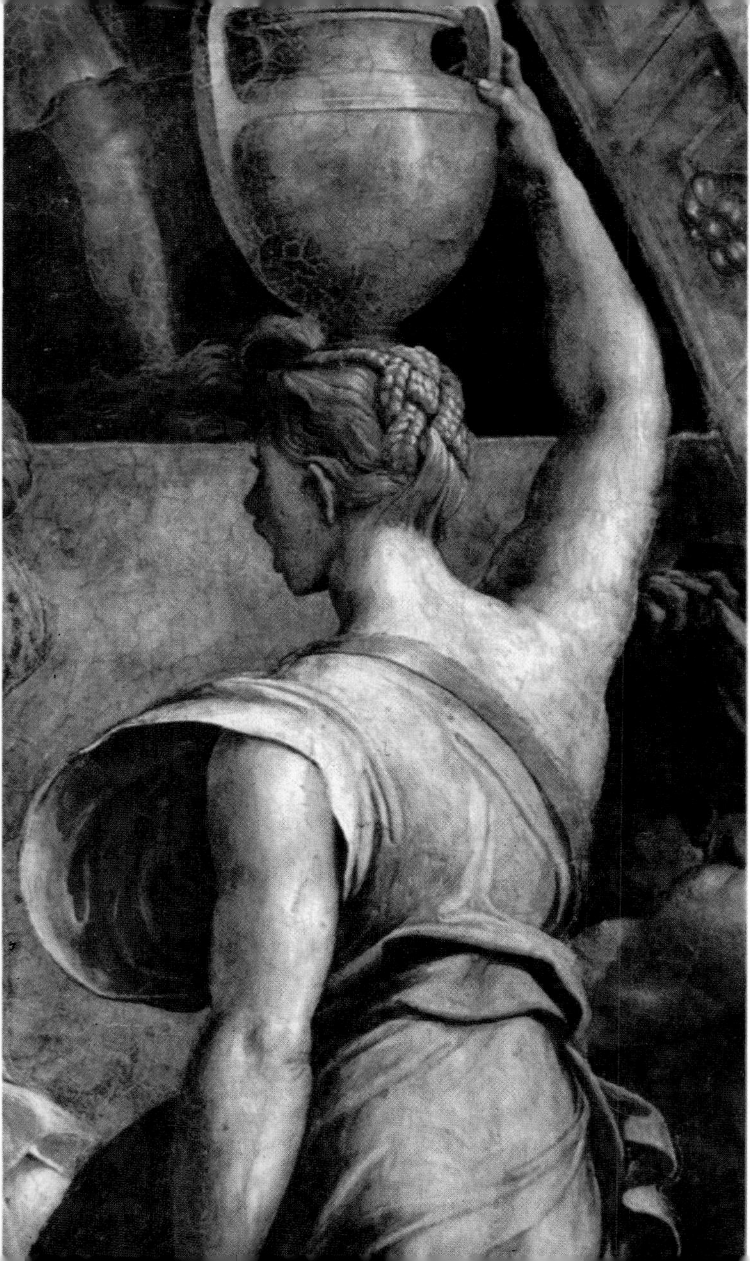

65

71

77

78

79